Bouncy B
Goes S

A shared reading Letterland play

Published 2005 by Letterland International Ltd
Barton, Cambridge, CB3 7AY, UK

Tel +44 (0)870 766 2629 or +44 (0)1223 262675
Fax +44 (0)1223 264126 • info@letterland

www.letterland.com

First published 2005
ISBN 1862093121
Product Code: T47B

Designed by Susi Martin-Taylor

British Library Cataloguing in Publication Data
A Catalogue record for this publication is available from the British Library

Printed in Hong Kong

Letterland

Bouncy Ben Goes Shopping

by Domenica Maxted

Illustrated by the Geri Livingston Studio

The Characters

Bouncy Ben

Oscar Orange

Harry Hat Man

Sammy Snake

Peter Puppy

Plus: Narrator and Chorus Leader

Bouncy Ben Goes Shopping

Narrator

In Letterland, one sunny day,
the Letterland friends go out to play.
But Bouncy Ben has a job to do
and he'll need lots of help – from you!

Bouncy Ben

My mummy has asked me to go to the shops. She's given me a list so I can remember what to buy.

[*Harry Hat Man comes in.*]

Harry Hat Man

Hello, Bouncy Ben! What are you doing?

Bouncy Ben

I'm going to the shops for my mummy. I've got to buy...

[*Reads from list.*]

eggs
butter
milk
cake

Narrator

Let's help Bouncy Ben remember everything. All together, let's all sing.

Chorus

eggs
butter
milk
cake

[*Peter Puppy and Oscar Orange come in.*]

Peter Puppy

Hello, Bouncy Ben. Let's play chase!

Bouncy Ben

But I've got to go shopping for my mummy.

Oscar Orange

Just a quick game. Please!

[Bouncy Ben drops his list as everyone runs off. Narrator picks it up.]

Narrator

Can you see what happened then?
A terrible thing for Bouncy Ben.
He has dropped his shopping list.
I wonder if it will be missed.

[Bouncy Ben, Harry Hat Man, Oscar Orange and Peter Puppy come back.]

Bouncy Ben

Oh no! Where is my list? How am I going to remember what to buy?

Harry Hat Man

I'll help you, Bouncy Ben. I think the first thing on the list began with the sound 'e...'.

Oscar Orange

Elephant?

Peter Puppy

Envelope?

Chorus

Eggs!

[*Narrator writes 'eggs' on a board.*]

Bouncy Ben

But what else did I have to get at the shops?

Harry Hat Man

I think the second thing began with the sound 'b...'.

Peter Puppy

Buttons?

Oscar Orange

Ball?

Chorus

Butter!

[*Narrator writes 'butter' on a board.*]

Bouncy Ben

Oh, thank you! But what else did I have to get?

Harry Hat Man

I think the third thing began with the sound 'mmm...'.

Oscar Orange

Magnet?

Peter Puppy

Mouse?

Chorus

Milk!

[*Narrator writes 'milk' on a board.*]

Bouncy Ben

Brilliant! That's everything.
Thank you!

Narrator

Bouncy Ben, not so fast.
You've forgotten the very last.

Bouncy Ben

Oh yes. And I think it was
something very nice.

Harry Hat Man

Something beginning with 'c...'.

Peter Puppy

Cat?

Bouncy Ben

No, it was something
nice to eat.

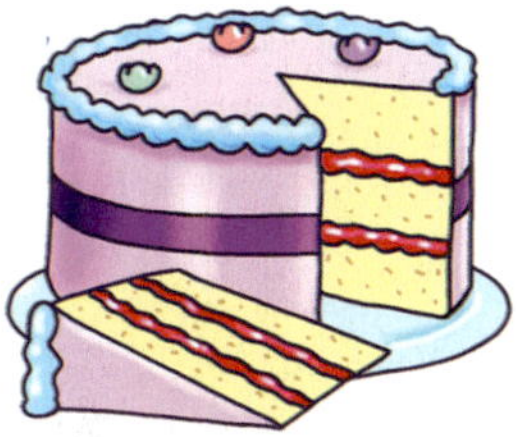

Chorus

Cake!

[*Narrator writes 'cake' on a board.*]

Narrator

All together, don't forget!
Let's tell Ben just what to get.

Chorus

eggs
butter
milk
cake

[*Sammy Snake comes in wearing an apron.*]

Sammy Snake

Hello, Bouncy Ben. Welcome to my shop.

Bouncy Ben

Hello, Sammy Snake. I would like to buy...

Bouncy Ben and Chorus

eggs
butter
milk
cake

Narrator

Don't forget the magic word!

Bouncy Ben

Please!

[*Puts things in a basket and hands them over.*]

Sammy Snake

There you are, Bouncy Ben.

Sammy Snake

That will be two Letterland coins, please.

Bouncy Ben

Thank you, Sammy Snake.
Here you are.

[*Takes the basket and hands over the money*].

Sammy Snake

Thank you. Goodbye.

Bouncy Ben

Goodbye.

Narrator

Now, Bouncy Ben is on his way but can he read what these letters say?

[*Sammy, Harry, Oscar and Peter stand in a line to form the word 'shop'.*]

Bouncy Ben

Can you help me?

Chorus

Shop!

Narrator

Well done, Ben. Well done, all of you!
Today you've learnt a thing or two –
how to shop and how to read,
and how to help a friend in need!

[*Note: See page 23 for the **sh** digraph story.*]

Tips for Teachers

This play can be used for a performance (in assembly or class), for group reading, or as part of your phonics teaching after learning the **sh** story – see page 23.

The play has six spoken parts, including the Narrator who can either be yourself or an older child. The other five parts are played by children – it doesn't matter if the characters are played by boys or girls. A sixth child can act as Chorus Leader, in charge of holding up the chorus cards (see opposite). This role provides a good opportunity for a less able reader to become fully involved in the activities. The Chorus consists of the rest of the class or the audience; alternatively, it could be spoken just by the characters in the play.

Bouncy Ben Goes Shopping is especially written to provide practice in literacy skills, including initial sounds, rhyming words, alliteration and word building. Reading or performing this play in groups helps improve speaking and listening skills as well as encouraging social and personal development.

Preparation

Before starting work on the play:

- Explain to the children how stories may be told in various ways, and that a 'play' allows them to pretend they're people in a story. Discuss how actors on TV and in films have to learn their words and rehearse their roles, as if acting in a play.

- Tell the children at the outset if the play is to be performed for an audience. If it is, this will help motivate everyone to re-read their parts until they have achieved real fluency and lively expression.

- Briefly, in your own words, tell the story of the play.

- Explain the special words used in relation to the play, for example, 'narrator', 'chorus', 'props'.

- Encourage the children to use plenty of expression when reading their parts.

- Write the chorus parts in large print on a series of cards, or a flipchart – your class may enjoy doing this themselves.

Props and costumes

Bouncy Ben Goes Shopping uses the following props: shopping list, whiteboard, apron for shopkeeper, shopping basket or bag and coins. You could also show the items that Ben buys in the shop (eggs, butter, milk, cake). Alternatively, children can mime using the relevant objects.

All the characters should have their letters, in lower case, on their chests or on headbands to help identify themselves to the audience. This will also allow them to form the 'live spelling' word at the end of the play. The *Letterland Big Picture Code Cards* are useful for this purpose because they will show up well at a distance.

In addition, the characters could also wear or carry the following costumes and props to help represent their Letterland characters:

Bouncy Ben: felt rabbit ears

Harry Hat Man: green hat

Oscar Orange: orange T-shirt, an orange

Peter Puppy: floppy felt puppy ears

Sammy Snake: headband with card or felt snake's head

Cross-curricular links

Bouncy Ben Goes Shopping provides plenty of opportunities for cross-curricular links, for example:

Numeracy: set up a class shop to practise adding and taking away, giving change, etc.

Literacy: write shopping lists; play memory games such as Kim's Game ("I went to the shops and I bought a…"), or put objects on a tray and see how many children can remember.

D&T: discuss food technology and making cakes.

Science: explore what happens when you heat materials (e.g. eggs) and how they change form.

The 'sh' Digraph Story

Use this play after you have taught the **sh** digraph story (see page 60-61 of the *Letterland Teacher's Guide*). As a reminder: Sammy Snake loves to hiss ('**sss**'), but Harry Hat Man hates noise, so he hushes Sammy with a '**sh**' sound!

Letterland

Learning with Letterland

Log on to the full range of Letterland titles at

www.letterland.com